HOW TO BE...

a CHEF

Stephanie Turnbull

A⁺

Smart Apple Media

Published by Smart Apple Media, an imprint of Black Rabbit Books
P.O. Box 3263, Mankato, Minnesota, 56002
www.blackrabbitbooks.com

Printed in the United States of America, at Corporate Graphics
in North Mankato, Minnesota.

Designed and illustrated by Guy Callaby
Edited by Mary-Jane Wilkins

Cataloging-in-Publication Data is available from the Library of Congress

ISBN 978-1-62588-366-7

Photo acknowledgements
t = top, b = bottom, c = center, l = left, r = right
page 1 ruzanna; 3t Galushko Sergey, l Dionisvera, r lazlo, b Africa Studio/all
Shutterstock; 4t Innershadows/Thinkstock, l design56, cl Bernd Schmidt,
c photosync, b Olga Kovalenko, br Shawn Hempel; 5t Montypeter, r Andrey
Armyagov, b Ariwasabi; 7 bitt24; 8 Toranico; 10 Garry L.; 11 Joe Gough;
12 Paul Cowan; 13 Paul Horwitz; 14 Denizo71; 18 Pablo Hidalgo; 19t Lilyana
Vynogradova, b Sally Scott/all Shutterstock; 20 sergeyskleznev;
21 robynmac/both Thinkstock; 22 Robyn Mackenzie; 23 DJ Taylor/
both Shutterstock
Cover Simone van den Berg/Shutterstock

DAD0060
022015
9 8 7 6 5 4 3 2 1

Contents

Starter skills

Cook amazing meals for your friends and family by starting with the brilliantly easy recipes in this book. Who knows, it could lead to a career as a famous chef!

Baking basics

Choose simple, tasty recipes and make sure you have all the ingredients and equipment you need before you start. If you're cooking for other people, check whether they're **vegetarian**, **vegan**, or have food **allergies**.

It's fun to spend time in the kitchen cooking up tasty treats.

Blender

Saucepans

Here is some basic cooking equipment you may need.

Wooden spoon

Grater

Colander

Safety first

Kitchens can be dangerous places, so remember these safety rules—and make sure an adult is on hand to help!

1 Wash your hands, tie back hair, roll up sleeves, wear an apron, and work on a clean surface.

2 Be careful with knives: keep your fingers out of the way, work slowly, and use a chopping board.

3 Don't touch electrical items with wet hands, and be careful with the blades.

4 Beware of hot stoves: use oven gloves and move full pans carefully.

5 Keep raw meat away from other foods, use a separate knife and chopping board, and wash your hands afterward.

HANDY HINTS

Look out for the thumbs up. Here you'll find tips to make your food look and taste even better.

This warning hand is for important safety facts.

Super soup

This easy-peasy pea soup uses healthy ingredients and tastes great served hot with crusty bread for dipping.

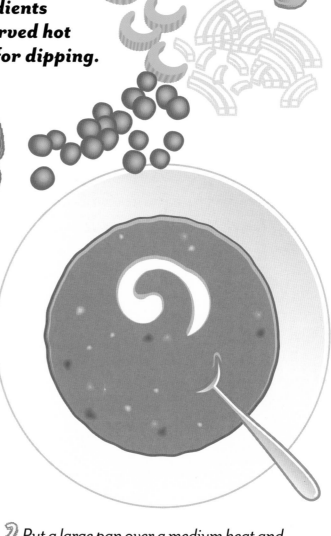

You will need
1 carrot
1 stick celery
1 onion
1 tbsp olive oil
1 vegetable or chicken **stock** cube
10 oz (400g) frozen peas
small bunch fresh mint

 Soup looks better with decoration on top! Try adding **croutons**, crumbled grilled bacon, or a swirl of cream.

1 Peel and slice the carrot. Wash and slice the celery and chop the onion.

2 Put a large pan over a medium heat and add the olive oil, then the carrot, celery, and onion. Mix with a wooden spoon and cook for about five minutes, stirring now and then.

3 Crumble the stock cube into a measuring jug and pour in 2 pints (1 l) of boiling water. Stir to dissolve the cube, then add to the pan.

4 Add the peas, bring the soup to the boil and let it **simmer** for ten minutes. Take the pan off the heat.

5 Pick and wash the mint leaves and add them to the pan with a sprinkle of salt and pepper.

6 Use a hand-held liquidizer to purée the mixture until it's fairly smooth, or whizz it up in a blender. Heat it again and serve.

WHAT NEXT? *Invent your own soups by gently frying chopped vegetables in a big pan, adding stock and herbs and leaving them to simmer. **Blend** them or leave them chunky.*

Your soup could contain chopped potato, tomato, sausage, or chicken.

Simple stir fry

Stir fries are quick, easy, all-in-one meals made in a big pan called a wok. Try this simple chicken chow mein—it's packed with healthy ingredients.

You will need

3 oz (75g) dried egg noodles per person

2 skinless chicken breasts

1 onion

2 cloves garlic

thumb-sized piece root ginger

handful snow peas, washed

small can water chestnuts

1 tbsp sunflower oil

2 handfuls beansprouts

3 tbsp soy sauce

2 tbsp sweet chili sauce

1 Cook the noodles in a pan of boiling water according to the packet instructions. Drain in a colander.

2 Cut the chicken breasts into thin, finger-length strips.

Remember the rules for handling raw meat (see page 5).

Root ginger

Water chestnuts

Garlic

Onion

Snow peas

3 Slice the onion and garlic, then peel and finely chop the ginger. Halve the snow peas lengthways. Drain and halve the water chestnuts.

4 Heat a wok over medium heat, then add the oil and chicken. Cook for five minutes, stirring.

Use a wooden spatula, not a metal spoon that will heat up.

If you don't have a wok, use a large pan.

5 Add the onion, garlic, and ginger. Stir fry for another two minutes.

6 Add the water chestnuts, bean sprouts, and noodles. Mix in the soy sauce and chili sauce and stir fry for a few minutes until hot. Serve into bowls and eat right away!

WHAT NEXT?
Try stir fries with other vegetables, such as baby sweetcorn, sliced zucchini, carrot sticks, and red pepper strips. Don't overcook them or they'll go soggy!

Cool curry

Curries are another easy meal made in one big pan. This creamy lamb and sweet potato coconut curry tastes great with rice or **naan**.

You will need

1 onion

2 cloves garlic

thumb-sized piece
  root ginger

1 lb 12 oz (800g)
  lean, cubed lamb

3 tbsp sunflower oil

2 tsp mild curry powder

1 tsp ground coriander

½ tsp ground
  cumin

1 can coconut milk

1 tbsp lime juice

2 medium sweet potatoes

dried coconut

1 Peel and chop the onion, garlic, and ginger.

2 Heat the oil in a large pan and add the curry powder, coriander, and cumin. Gently cook, stirring, for a minute.

3 Add the garlic, ginger, and onion and fry for five minutes, stirring.

4 Stir in the lamb, coconut milk, and lime juice, and add a sprinkle of salt and pepper. Bring the mixture gently to a boil and simmer for 20 minutes, stirring a few times.

5 *Peel and chop the sweet potato into roughly 1 inch (2.5 cm) cubes. Add to the curry and simmer for 25 minutes.*

6 *Serve with a sprinkle of dried coconut.*

Cook rice according to the package's instructions.

 *Add a little more curry powder if you prefer your curries hot!*

WHAT NEXT? *Spice up rice by adding a teaspoon of bright yellow* **turmeric** *as it simmers. You could also fry a few flaked almonds in butter, then stir them into the cooked rice.*

Brilliant burgers

Burgers in buns are great for parties. You can make them with ground beef or lamb, or why not try these cool *falafel* burgers?

You will need
(to make 4 burgers)
2 cans chickpeas
1 red onion
2 cloves garlic
handful flat leaf parsley, washed
1 tsp ground coriander
1 tsp ground cumin
½ tsp chili powder
1 tsp lemon juice
2 tbsp plain flour
1 tbsp sunflower oil

1 Drain the chickpeas well.

2 Peel and chop the red onion and garlic cloves. Chop the parsley.

3 Put the chickpeas and chopped ingredients in a blender. Add the coriander, cumin, chili, lemon juice, flour, and a sprinkle of salt and pepper. Blend until well-mixed but not completely smooth.

4 On a floury surface, shape the mixture into burgers.

5 Heat the oil in a frying pan and fry the burgers for a few minutes on each side. Turn them with a spatula.

6 Serve the warm burgers in buns. Add extras such as lettuce, cucumber slices, and strips of roasted red peppers (which you can buy in a jar).

 Add a dollop of salsa, plain yogurt, or sour cream.

WHAT NEXT? Try shaping falafel into small balls and serving it in pita bread pockets with salad and **tzatziki**. Delicious!

Perfect pizza

Making your own pizza dough isn't as hard as you might think–and it's fun to try different toppings.

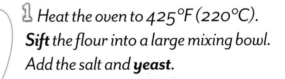

You will need (for 4 pizzas)
1 lb (450 g) bread flour
1 ⅓ cups (300 ml) warm water
1 package dried **yeast**
1 tbsp olive oil
1 tsp salt
can of pizza sauce
choice of toppings

Expert pizza makers flip and spin dough to shape and stretch it.

1 Heat the oven to 425°F (220°C). **Sift** the flour into a large mixing bowl. Add the salt and **yeast**.

2 Make a hollow in the middle and pour in the warm water and olive oil.

Don't use hot or boiling water, or your dough won't rise.

3 Mix until smooth with a wooden spoon. Add a few drops of water if it's dry, or a sprinkling of bread flour if it's sticky.

4 Put the dough on a floury surface and **knead** it for ten minutes. Push it away, then pull it back and fold it over itself. Keep turning the dough as you knead. It will become smooth and stretchy.

5 Put the dough back in the bowl and cover with a dish towel. Set it in a warm place for an hour and a half. It will double in size!

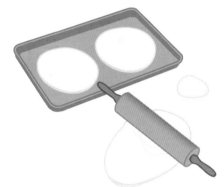

Each pizza should be less than a ½ inch (1 cm) thick.

6 Divide the risen dough into four pieces and roll them out on a floury surface.

7 Smooth a tablespoon of pizza sauce over each base, then add toppings. Try slices of mozzarella cheese, pepperoni, green peppers, mushrooms, cubed ham, pineapple, olives, or tomatoes.

8 Bake in a pre-heated oven at 425°C (220°C for about 12 minutes, until the edges are golden.

WHAT NEXT? Hold a pizza party! Make the dough beforehand and store it in the fridge, wrapped in cling film. Put out bowls of toppings and let friends design their own pizzas.

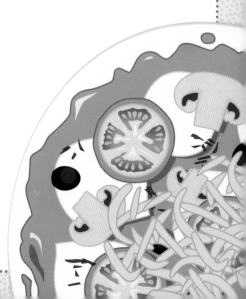

Speedy pudding

A good cook needs a great dessert to finish off a fantastic meal. Try this easy pudding—it only takes seven minutes to cook in a microwave!

You will need
4 oz (100g) butter
4 oz (100g) fine sugar
2 medium eggs
2 tbsp milk
4 oz (100g) self-raising flour
1 orange
8 tbsp golden syrup

1 Put the butter and sugar in a bowl and blend them together with a wooden spoon until smooth.

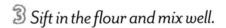

2 In a separate bowl, whisk the eggs and milk, then stir into the butter and sugar mixture.

3 Sift in the flour and mix well.

4 Grate the orange zest (skin) into the mixture, then cut the orange in half and squeeze in the juice of one half.

 Stop grating when you reach the bitter white layer (the pith) under the skin.

5 *Draw around the top of a large microwave bowl on parchment paper. Cut out the circle.*

6 *Grease the bowl with a little butter or margarine, then spoon in the syrup. Pour the pudding mixture on top. Grease the circle of paper and put it on top, butter side down.*

7 *Cook in a microwave for seven minutes on medium power, then let it stand for a few minutes. Remove the paper, put a plate over the dish, and turn everything upside down so the pudding falls on to the plate. Serve hot.*

WHAT NEXT? *Try making this pudding with maple syrup or jam, or add a few raisins to the mixture. Or make individual puddings in tea cups!*

Hot fruit feast

For a sweet but healthy dessert, try baked fruit. Apples bake well, and you don't need to peel or chop them.

You will need

4 large apples

4 tbsp dark brown sugar

1 tsp mixed spice

handful white raisins

handful chopped pecans or walnuts

4 tsp butter

1 Preheat the oven to 400°F (200°C). Wash the apples and remove the cores. Stand them in a baking dish.

An apple corer is useful for this.

2 In a bowl, mix the dark brown sugar, mixed spice, raisins, and nuts.

3 Fill the cored apples with the mixture and sprinkle any extra around the dish. Put a teaspoon of butter on each apple and pour a little water into the dish—make it about ¼ inch (5 mm) deep.

4 *Bake on a low rack of the oven for 15 minutes, then spoon some of the liquid over the apples. Put back in the oven for another 10-15 minutes. Serve the apples in bowls and pour the extra juice on top.*

Vanilla ice cream goes very well with baked fruit.

Apple crumble is a great mix of soft fruit and crunchy topping.

WHAT NEXT?

Try making an apple crumble by mixing 2 oz (55g) butter into 4 oz (110g) flour and 2 oz (55g) sugar until it looks like bread crumbs. Sprinkle the mixture over a dish of chopped apples and bake for about 30 minutes at 400°F (200°C).

Quick cookies

Warm cookies make perfect mid-afternoon snacks or party treats. Start with these simple chocolate chip cookies.

You will need
4½ oz (125g) butter
2 oz (55g) sugar
6 oz (165g) plain flour
2 oz (55g) chocolate chips, or broken-up chocolate

1 Heat the oven to 325°F 170°C. In a bowl, blend the butter and sugar with a wooden spoon until smooth.

2 Stir in the plain flour and mix to a smooth dough. Stir in the chocolate chips.

3 Shape the dough into a fat sausage, wrap it in cling film, and chill in the fridge for 20 minutes.

Your cookies will be chewy when warm. They soon turn hard, so store them in an airtight box.

4 Cut the dough into thick circles and arrange on a greased baking tray. Cook for 10-15 minutes until they're a pale golden color.

5 Remove from the oven and use a spatula to transfer them carefully to a wire rack to cool.

Cookies may bake faster than you think, so don't let them burn. If they do, make a note so you get it right next time!

WHAT NEXT? Try making cookies without chocolate chips and cover them in icing instead. Or roll out the dough and create shapes with cookie cutters rather than cutting into circles.

Glossary

allergy
A sensitivity to something which leads to reactions such as sneezing and skin rashes, or sometimes even dizziness and difficulty breathing.

blend
To mix ingredients together until smooth. You can blend with a spoon or an electric blender.

crouton
A small, crunchy cube of dried bread. You can make your own croutons or buy them in packages.

falafel
falafel
A Middle Eastern food made from chickpeas. It's low in fat and a healthy alternative to meat.

knead
To push, pull, and fold dough in a way that makes it full of air so that it rises when it cooks.

naan
A flat bread from south and central Asia. Some naan contain fillings such as raisins, onion, or coconut.

sift
To get rid of lumps in dry ingredients by putting them through a plastic or metal sifter. Sifters have lots of tiny holes that you can shake or press grains through.

simmer
To keep liquid cooking gently, with just a few bubbles, not boiling fiercely.

stock
Water flavored with meat, vegetables, herbs, or spices. Some cooks make their own stock, but the easiest method is to dissolve dried stock cubes in hot water.

turmeric
A south Asian plant that is dried and ground into a peppery, orange powder.

turmeric

tzatziki
A Greek and Turkish dip made of yogurt, cucumber, and mint.

vegan
Someone who doesn't eat any food that comes from animals, including meat, eggs, and dairy products.

vegetarian
Someone who doesn't eat meat.

whisk
To mix fast with a hand whisk, fork, or electric whisk to whip air into ingredients.

yeast
A fungus that creates air bubbles in dough when warmed. Without yeast, your pizza bases would be flat and hard!

Websites

www.schoolfamily.com/recipes/category/recipes-kids-can-make-alone
Find lots of easy, delicious recipes to make and eat.

vegetarian.about.com
Learn about vegetarian and vegan diets and discover inventive recipes using vegetables.

careerplanning.about.com/od/occupations/p/chef_cook.htm
Take a quiz to see whether you have the right skills to be a chef, then read about cooking careers.

Index